Coyote's Magic

by Joyce A. Churchill
illustrated by David Sheldon

Scott Foresman
is an imprint of

Glenview, Illinois • Boston, Massachusetts • Mesa, Arizona
Shoreview, Minnesota • Upper Saddle River, New Jersey

Every effort has been made to secure permission and provide appropriate credit for photographic material. The publisher deeply regrets any omission and pledges to correct errors called to its attention in subsequent editions.

Unless otherwise acknowledged, all photographs are the property of Pearson.

Photo locations denoted as follows: Top (T), Center (C), Bottom (B), Left (L), Right (R), Background (Bkgd)

Illustrations by David Sheldon

Photograph 24 DK Images

ISBN 13: 978-0-328-39429-6
ISBN 10:   0-328-39429-7

Chapter One

"Hurry up!" Maggie called. "You're going to miss the camp bus!"

Henry Samuels was tired of his little sister telling him what to do. Maggie was seven and a half, which made her more than a year younger than Henry, who was now nine.

Henry thought about how different their interests were. He liked building model airplanes and learning about history. His sister liked to sing and dance in her school plays, and she was very interested in animals.

Maggie often went with their mother to the Southwest Colorado Animal Shelter in the nearby town of Hesperus. They helped care for the homeless animals there.

Henry couldn't bear to face all those yelping dogs, with their sharp teeth and unpleasant smells. If he had his way, he would never see another dog for the rest of his life! He was terribly afraid of them.

Henry's stomach turned as he thought of his fear of dogs, and he could barely eat his breakfast!

His mother's voice brought Henry to attention. "Quit daydreaming, Henry. The camp bus is already here to take you to the museum," she said. In between thinking about his sister and the dogs at the animal shelter, Henry had totally forgotten about today's summer camp field trip! He raced out of the house towards the bus, trailing far behind Maggie.

Now she'll call me slow for being late to the bus, Henry thought.

By the time Henry reached the bus, he was panting and almost out of breath. His friend Tommy waved to him as he stepped aboard. Tommy was nine, the same age as Henry. He was tall and thin and had dark black hair, and he was a chatterbox. He was interested in everything, and he liked to talk about everything. Tommy didn't even care if people were listening to him. He just liked to talk.

"Remind me to walk Skipper when I get home today," Tommy said, as Henry sat down next to him in the seat.

Henry avoided Tommy's big, black dog, Skipper, whenever he was over at his house. Sometimes the two boys practiced magic tricks together. Tommy was a good assistant, and the two boys had fun performing their tricks.

"Is this going to be a cool summer or what?" Tommy asked with excitement. "I can't wait to get to the museum."

"Today's program is supposed to be all about storytelling," Maggie chimed in from the seat behind them. "I bet there will be a Navajo storyteller."

The bus bounced along the road, kicking up clouds of red-clay dust. After swirling through the air, the dust settled on the dry shrubs and bean fields that dotted the roadside. Henry tuned out Tommy's voice and listened to the hum of the wheels until they turned into the entrance of Mesa Verde National Park.

The bus rambled past the campground and the visitor center. Henry could see Cliff Palace, the park's largest cliff dwelling. It was built by the ancient Pueblo people. Henry and Maggie had explored it last year with their parents. They had walked through its twelve-foot tunnel and marveled at the thirty-two-foot ladder that went to the top dwelling.

Chapter Two

Henry was full of excitement as he got off the bus and walked into the museum with the other children. He was anxious to learn more about the people who had left behind Mesa Verde's incredible ruins. When they reached the museum classroom, a man named Lonnie Gordon was waiting for them.

Mr. Gordon explained that he was a descendant of a Navajo storyteller. He was young, with dark eyes and a bright smile. Mr. Gordon's dark hair was pushed under a colorful headband that was knotted at the back of his head.

"My great-great-grandfather was a Navajo storyteller," Mr. Gordon began. "At night, when my brothers and I were young, we would sit around the campfire and hear the stories of our forefathers. Now I'm going to tell you some stories about a special animal, Coyote. He is unique to the Navajo culture.

"Sometimes Coyote helped our people, but other times he played tricks on us."

Mr. Gordon then told several stories about the Coyote and his cunning ways.

"One of Great-Great-Grandfather's favorite stories was about how Coyote stole fire." Mr. Gordon leaned closer and said, "It's one of my favorite stories too."

How Coyote Stole Fire

Mr. Gordon began, "Coyote had no need for fire. His fur kept him warm in the winter.

"One day as he passed a village, he heard a man talking. 'The Sun is warm on my back,' the man said. 'It warms the earth and makes stones hot to the touch. If only we could have a small piece of the Sun to heat our shelters during winter, we could stay warm.'

"Coyote felt sorry for the villagers because they were hairless and not protected from the wind and cold. He knew where the Fire Beings lived in the mountains, and he decided to go to the mountains to steal fire for the villagers."

Mr. Gordon continued, "Coyote crept up the mountain. The Fire Beings, sitting in their mountaintop lair, spotted him from a long way away. But what did they have to fear from one lone gray coyote? They paid him little attention.

"Coyote watched all day as the Fire Beings fed fuel to their fire, and he was still watching as the Fire Beings guarded the fire deep into the night.

"Coyote knew that the Fire Beings changed guards at dawn, so he waited and was ready. At the moment when the fire was left unguarded, Coyote scampered from the bushes, snatched a stick of fire, and ran down the mountainside as fast as he could. The Fire Beings saw him and began to chase him."

Mr. Gordon suddenly stopped speaking.

"Oh, I'm sorry," Mr. Gordon said. "We'll have to stop for today. I didn't realize the time, and I almost forgot that I have informational packages about coyotes for each of you to take home to read."

Mr. Gordon passed out the packages, and then he added, "There's one more thing. Please write down any questions you have for me and leave them at my office tomorrow. I hope you liked the tales of Coyote!"

Then the children went outside and climbed onto the bus for the ride home. They were excited about Mr. Gordon and the stories he had told.

When Henry got home he went straight to his room and opened up the coyote package. Inside were a brochure and a small poster of a coyote.

Henry eagerly examined the poster. It showed a coyote standing proudly on top of a mountain looking down onto the valley below. Its bushy, gray tail pointed straight down, and its pointy ears and yellow eyes were alert. The poster also contained some facts about coyotes and a drawing of a coyote pawprint. As much as Henry feared dogs, he thought that this coyote was neat, and he liked looking at it.

Henry carefully pinned the poster to the wall in his room.

Chapter Three

The next day, Henry, Maggie, Tommy, and the rest of the kids in their summer camp were back at the museum. This time, they went to a junior archaeology explorer class. They looked at artifacts that had been dug up in the park. Henry studied clues under the microscope and looked at pieces of ancient pottery.

On the computer, Henry played a game that allowed him to experience what it is like to dig at an archaeological site. The game was fun, but it wasn't nearly as exciting as hearing the story about Coyote from Mr. Gordon.

At the end of the day Henry wrote down a question for Mr. Gordon and marched down the hall to his office. Just as he arrived, the door swung wide open.

"Oh, hi. I remember you," said Mr. Gordon. "You were here yesterday. What's your name?"

"Henry."

"Well, Henry, are you coming back tomorrow to hear the rest of Coyote's tale?" asked Mr. Gordon.

"Oh, yes. I want …" Henry froze when he felt something wet against his hand. Staring up at him was the biggest, toughest-looking dog that he had ever seen! Henry was terrified!

"This is Ranger, my coydog," Mr. Gordon explained.

Henry could barely talk, he was so afraid. Finally, he stammered, "What … is a coydog?"

"Ranger is part dog and part coyote," Mr. Gordon answered, trying to calm Henry. "You'll see him tomorrow at the storytelling."

Henry backed away because he couldn't bear to touch Ranger. He hurried down the hall and out the front door to the bus. When he got to his seat next to Tommy, he realized his question was still in his hand, squeezed into a tight lump. He listened to Tommy jabbering about the archaeology computer game.

"Did you see Mr. Gordon today?" Maggie interrupted. "He has a cool dog named Ranger that looks just like a coyote. I loved Ranger so much that I wanted to bring him home!"

"Yeah, I saw him," Henry replied. He refused to let his sister know how afraid he had been, and he said no more on the matter.

In his dreams that night Henry was running down a mountainside with fierce Fire Beings chasing him. When the Fire Beings got too close, Henry turned and breathed fire on them!

Chapter Four

When the bus arrived at Mesa Verde the next morning, Mr. Gordon and Ranger were waiting for the children outside the museum. Once they were settled in the classroom, Mr. Gordon introduced Ranger to them and explained about coydogs. Then Ranger settled at his feet, and Mr. Gordon continued his story.

How Coyote Stole Fire (continued)

"When we left off with our story," Mr. Gordon began, "Coyote was escaping from the Fire Beings. They were close behind, chasing him down the mountain."

Mr. Gordon went on: "One of the Fire Beings reached out and touched the tip of Coyote's tail, and the tail fur turned white!

"Coyote cried out and flung the fire he was carrying away from him. Squirrel, who just happened to be sitting on the mountaintop the entire time, caught the burning stick. She put it on her back and ran through the trees. The fire scorched her back, and Squirrel curled up her tail in a desperate attempt to put out the fire. Even now, squirrels have tails that curl over their backs!

"Squirrel threw the fire to Chipmunk, who had no idea that a chase had been going on. She was afraid and froze in place until the Fire Beings had almost reached her. As she turned away, a Fire Being reached out and clawed at her back, leaving three stripes! To this day, chipmunks have striped backs.

"Chipmunk threw the fire to Frog. The Fire Being grabbed at Frog's tail, but Frog gave a mighty leap and tore himself free, leaving his tail behind!

"Frog threw the fire to Wood, who swallowed it and refused to give it back to the Fire Beings. Finally, admitting defeat, the Fire Beings retreated back up the mountain."

Mr. Gordon continued: "Coyote knew how to get the fire out of Wood. He went to the villagers and showed them how to rub two sticks together or rub a sharpened stick in a hole made in another piece of Wood. Because of Coyote's ability to tease fire out of Wood, humans never had to worry about being cold in the winter ever again." Mr. Gordon beamed when he had finished the story.

Chapter Five

After lunch the children returned to the museum classroom. "I have more stories about Coyote for you to take home," Mr. Gordon told them. "Who will help me pass them out?"

Henry raised his hand. "Henry, come on up," Mr. Gordon said. For a brief moment Henry had forgotten about Ranger, who was still lying at Mr. Gordon's feet.

When he saw Ranger, Henry's fear of dogs took over, but he willed himself to walk up to the front of the room and stand next to the coydog. Mr. Gordon signaled Ranger to get up. Then he showed the children Ranger's pointed ears and white underparts.

"It's OK," Mr. Gordon said. "Ranger likes to be petted. Go on, Henry." Henry forced himself to reach down and touch the dog's bushy tail.

"The tip of his tail is white, just like the tip of Coyote's tail in the story," Mr. Gordon pointed out. Ranger wagged his tail and nuzzled Henry, who carefully patted the coydog's head. On the bus ride home, Henry was still trembling with excitement. He had made a breakthrough. Thanks to Ranger, he was no longer afraid of dogs!

The next morning Henry poured milk over his cereal. Then he looked up at his mother, who was washing strawberries at the sink.

"Is it possible . . ." Henry's voice trailed off and he started again. "Could I go with you and Maggie the next time you go to the animal shelter?"

Henry's mother turned from the sink to look at him in surprise. "But Henry, I thought you were terrified of dogs!" she said in astonishment.

"Well, I got to know this dog called Ranger over at Mesa Verde Park. Except he's not really a dog. He's a coydog," Henry replied, beaming.

"That sounds interesting," Henry's mother said, with a slightly puzzled expression on her face. "But what's a coydog?"

Henry smiled. "I think that's a story for another day."

Mesa Verde National Park

Mesa verde means "green table" in Spanish. Mesa Verde National Park is located high above the countryside in southwestern Colorado.

Mesa Verde was the home of the early Pueblo people, who lived there more than seven hundred years ago. Some were called cliff dwellers because they built their homes into the red clay cliffs.

Our government created the national park system to protect places like Mesa Verde from being destroyed. National parks are open to the public. There are exhibits to see and special programs to join. Many national parks have picnic grounds or camping areas.